CLIMATE Change

PROBLEMS and PROGRESS

Preserving Energy

CLIMATE Change
PROBLEMS and PROGRESS

CLIMATE Change
PROBLEMS and PROGRESS

Preserving Energy

James Shoals

Mason Crest

Mason Crest
450 Parkway Drive, Suite D
Broomall, PA 19008
www.masoncrest.com

Printed and bound in the United States of America.

Series ISBN: 978-1-4222-4353-4
Hardback ISBN: 978-1-4222-4360-2
EBook ISBN: 978-1-4222-7455-2

First printing
1 3 5 7 9 8 6 4 2

Cover photographs by Dreamstime.com: Weerapat Kiatdumrong (bottom); Speyeder (right); Sashkinw (left); Anna Om (bkgd).

Library of Congress Cataloging-in-Publication Data
Names: Shoals, James, author. Title: Preserving energy / by James Shoals.
Description: Broomall, PA : Mason Crest, [2020] | Series: Climate challenges: problems and progress | Includes bibliographical references and index.
Identifiers: LCCN 2019013878| ISBN 9781422243534 (series) | ISBN 9781422243602 (hardback) |
    ISBN 9781422274552 (ebook)
Subjects: LCSH: Energy conservation--Juvenile literature. | Power resources--Juvenile literature.
Classification: LCC TJ163.35 .S56 2020 | DDC 333.79/16--dc23 LC record available at https://lccn.loc.gov/2019013878

QR Codes disclaimer:

CONTENTS

KEY ICONS TO LOOK FOR

Words to Understand: These words with their easy-to-understand definitions will increase the reader's understanding of the text, while building vocabulary skills.

Sidebars: This boxed material within the main text allows readers to build knowledge, gain insights, explore possibilities, and broaden their perspectives by weaving together additional information to provide realistic and holistic perspectives.

Educational Videos: Readers can view videos by scanning our QR codes, providing them with additional educational content to supplement the text. Examples include news coverage, moments in history, speeches, iconic moments, and much more!

Text-Dependent Questions: These questions send the reader back to the text for more careful attention to the evidence presented here.

Research Projects: Readers are pointed toward areas of further inquiry connected to each chapter. Suggestions are provided for projects that encourage deeper research and analysis.

Series Glossary of Key Terms: This back-of-the-book glossary contains terminology used throughout this series. Words found here increase the reader's ability to read and comprehend higher-level books and articles in this field.

bowhead whales large-mouthed Arctic whale

catastrophic extremely harmful

copier electrical machine that makes copies of typed, written, or drawn material

curb to lessen the intensity of something

decompose break down

efficient being effective without wasting time, effort, or expense

endangered in immediate danger of extinction

fertilizer any substance, such as manure, used to increase soil fertility

generator an engine that converts mechanical energy into electrical energy

greenhouse gas a gas that contributes to the greenhouse effect by absorbing infrared radiation

iceberg a large mass of ice floating on sea

kilowatt-hour a unit of energy equal to the power of 1,000 watts operating for one hour

kinetic energy the mechanical energy that a body possesses due to its own motion

landfill a low area where waste is buried between the layers of earth

migrating moving periodically or seasonally

neutron an elementary particle with zero charge and the same mass as that of a proton; enters into the structure of the atomic nucleus

oil spill a thin film of oil floating on the top of water

pesticide a chemical used to kill pests, such as insects

precious of high worth or cost

remote something that can't be accessed and is lightly populated

seabed the bottom of a sea or ocean

solar cell a cell that converts solar energy into electrical energy

steeply in a steep manner (a sharp rise or fall)

sustainable capable of being sustained

thermostat a device for regulating temperature automatically by starting or stopping the supply of heat

ultimately as the end result of a process

unbleached not artificially colored or bleached

windbreak a fence of trees designed to lessen the force of wind

INTRODUCTION

A large percentage of electricity and fuels is generated by burning fossil fuels, which release harmful greenhouse gases (GHGs). GHGs cause and increase global warming. In order to reduce these harmful emissions, it is necessary to start saving energy. Moreover, fossil fuels are nonrenewable sources of energy and they are not going to last forever. In the near future, there will be no fossil fuels to generate electricity and fuel. Hence, it is important that we now look for alternative energy sources for the future.

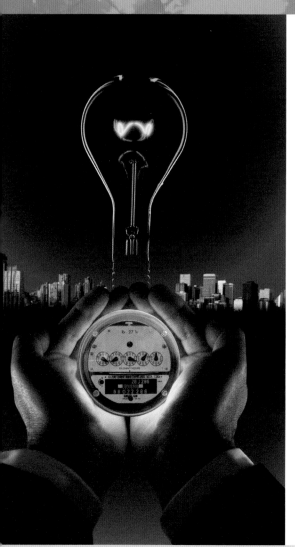

What is Energy?

Energy is the ability or capacity to do work. We use energy for lighting homes and cities, powering vehicles, and running factories and industries. Once industries were set up, the energy from fossil fuels came to be used widely. However, the overuse of fossil fuels for generating energy is increasing global warming.

Sources of Energy

Energy is obtained from various sources and is used in different forms. Living things obtain energy from the sun in the form of heat and light. Nonliving things such as machines and vehicles get energy from fuels like gasoline, diesel, electricity, and others.

Electricity

Electricity is the most widely used form of energy. It became available to us a few hundred years ago, and is now an integral part of our daily lives. We run our washing machines, televisions, refrigerators, air conditioners, and other appliances, with the help of electricity. At present, it is widely generated in fossil fuel power plants. However, due to increasing pollution and decreasing fossil fuels, hydropower, wind power, solar power, and nuclear power are being used to generate energy.

Gasoline and Diesel

All over the world, gasoline and diesel are the largest energy sources for running vehicles of all types. They are produced by refining crude oil in oil refineries. These oil refineries emit large amounts of greenhouse gases that cause global warming. In order to **curb** global warming, it is necessary to save energy and start finding replacements for these energy-dense and easily transportable fuels.

Climate Facts

- Energy cannot be destroyed; it just changes its form.

- Every year in the US, more than 2,300 million tons of carbon dioxide (CO_2) are produced by burning oil.

Sources of Energy

Renewable and nonrenewable are the two types of sources throug[h] which usable forms of energy are produced. Nonrenewable sources ar[e] those that cannot be replenished in a short period. Renewable source[s] are those that can be reproduced through natural processes.

Fossil Fuels

Natural gas, coal, and crude oil are foss[il] fuels, which are the most popularly use[d] nonrenewable energy sources. These wer[e] formed more than 300 million years ago b[y] the heat and pressure from the earth's cor[e] on the fossils (remains) of dead plants an[d] animals.

Uranium (Nuclear Energy)

The element uranium is also a nonrenewable source of energy. It[s] atoms are split through a process called nuclear fission to produc[e] energy. The production of energy from uranium is a cleaner pr[o]cess as compared to the production of energy by fossil fuels. How[-] ever, it is an expensive process.

Renewable Sources

There are five types of renewable energy sources.

- **Solar energy:** energy from the sun in the form of heat and light.
- **Hydro energy:** the **kinetic energy** of water.
- **Wind energy:** the energy developed from strong winds.
- **Geothermal energy:** the energy produced from the heat inside Earth.
- **Biomass energy:** the energy produced from plants and trees. Fuels like ethanol and biodiesel are made of corn and vegetable oil respectively.

Climate Facts

- All fossil fuels were formed in the Carboniferous Period, which occurred from about 360 to 286 million years ago.

- In 2011, about 91 percent of all energy used in the United States was produced from nonrenewable sources and about 4 percent from renewable sources.

Electricity Generation

Fossil fuels, nuclear energy, solar energy, wind, water, and biomass are the primary sources of energy. When energy from these sources is converted into a more usable form, they become secondary sources of energy. We depend heavily on fossil fuels for electricity.

Thermal Power Stations

In thermal power plants, electricity is generated by burning coal. The burned coal heats up the water in the boiler and produces steam. The steam flows into a turbine which spins the **generator** attached to it and generates electricity. However, the burning of coal emits large amounts of CO_2 into the atmosphere. These power plants are the major source of power in most countries of the world.

How electricity is generated

Other Power Stations

If we are to control global warming, it is essential to produce electricity through other means that do not release harmful GHGs.

- **Solar power plants:** Solar energy is converted into electricity through various means, such as **solar cells** and panels, etc.
- **Hydroelectric power plants:** Electricity is generated when the flow of water is used to turn the turbines of an electric generator at a dam.
- **Nuclear power plants:** Heat is produced by a process called nuclear fission. The atoms of uranium fuel split when hit by **neutrons**, releasing a large amount of heat that spins the turbines to generate electricity.
- **Wind power plants:** Electricity is generated when strong winds turn the windmills connected to the turbines of the electric generator.

Climate Facts

- The first public power station, the Edison Electric Light Station, was constructed in 1882 in New York City.

- About 20 percent of the world's electricity is generated in hydroelectric power plants.

Oil and Natural Gas Drilling

Precious energy sources such as crude oil and natural gas lie below the Earth's surface. Crude oil or petroleum is a smelly, yellow-black liquid that is also known as "black gold." Natural gas primarily consists of methane, CO_2, nitrogen, and hydrogen sulfide. Their extraction incurs not only huge energy costs but it also releases pollutants into the atmosphere.

Oil Drilling

Crude oil lies in rocks found deep within the layers of land and **seabed**. Experts first study the layers of rocks and then search for locations where they are likely to find the oil. The process of oil drilling requires a lot of energy. The rig set up for drilling is fitted with electric motors and electrical generators, which consume a lot of energy when holes are drilled and the oil is pumped out. It is then processed, and transported through tankers and pipelines to oil refineries. These processes also require energy.

Pollution and Warming

Crude oil is refined in oil refineries to produce important fuels such as kerosene, gasoline, diesel, LPG (liquefied petroleum gas), etc. Natural gas is burned to produce electricity, cook food, and other heating purposes. However, oil and natural gas refineries release enormous amounts of greenhouse gases that contribute to global warming.

Natural Gas Extraction

Though it is one of the most environment-friendly fossil fuels, the exploration, production, and transportation of natural gas involve considerable energy costs. Electric power is required to drill wells in gas fields, after which the gas is sent to a processing plant where its impurities are filtered out and it is further separated into its various components. Miles and miles of underground pipelines are needed to transport the gas to its final destination. These processes incur the expenditure of valuable energy.

Climate Facts

• Saudi Arabia and many other countries in the Middle East have about half of the world's oil reserves.

• The United States is the world's largest producer of natural gas.

Arctic Oil Drilling

t is estimated that almost a quarter of the Earth's undiscovered oil lies in the ocean floor of the Arctic Circle. Oil companies have turned towards the Arctic Ocean's unspoiled waters for oil drilling. However, Arctic oil drilling poses huge risks to both native life and the environment.

High Risk Enterprise

The Arctic is a **remote** location with freezing temperatures and extreme weather. It is very dangerous to work in such conditions. The presence of **icebergs** greatly increases the risks involved in oil drilling. Huge ships have to be used to move the icebergs out of the way; in some situations, the drilling has to be stopped and moved out of the way of icebergs the size of cities.

Dangers

Drilling for oil in the Arctic is not without its pitfalls. There are possibilities of damage to life under water, the local Eskimo communities who depend on native animals for survival, wildlife, and the Arctic ecosystem. An oil company likely to drill in the Arctic has even developed a new technology to reduce drilling noise.

Possibility of Oil Spill

Arctic oil drilling is an issue of major concern due to the possibility of an **oil spill** under the frozen area. Until now, no technology has been developed that could clean up an oil spill in frozen areas. An oil spill in the Arctic would have **catastrophic** effect on the local fisheries and the environment. It would affect millions of **migrating** birds, species of seabirds, polar bears, seals, arctic foxes, and **bowhead whales**.

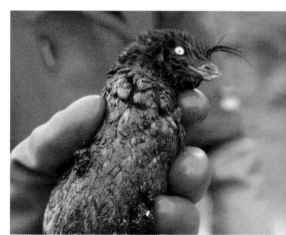

Climate Facts

- About four million people live in the Arctic region.

- The US Geological Survey states that around 13 percent of the world's undiscovered oil might be lying under the area north of the Arctic Circle.

Energy and Global Warming

CO$_2$ is the major GHG contributing to the rising global temperatures. It is released in large amounts during the production of electricity, the process of refining oil, and the burning of fuels in vehicles. Therefore, we need to save energy to reduce CO$_2$ emissions and control global warming.

Electrical Pollution

Electricity is generated by burning fossil fuels in power plants. The more electricity we use, the more air pollution it creates that heightens global warming. We cause electrical pollution by keeping the appliances switched on when not in use. This type of pollution is the cause of many health problems, such as cardiac and neurological disorders.

Industrial Pollution

Since the 1700s, coal has been burned to meet the energy demands of industries around the world. Today, there are more industries in the world than ever. The industrial fumes and waste is a leading cause of global warming. The use of packaged materials produced by industries should be discouraged since their production process is responsible for releasing large amounts of GHGs.

Transport Pollution

Oil is another widely used form of energy. Fuel is derived after refining the oil. With the increasing number of vehicles on the road, the rate of oil consumption is also increasing. During the oil-refining process, CO_2 is released into the air. When vehicles burn fuel, other **greenhouse gases** are also released into the air along with CO_2. These emissions contribute to global warming.

Climate Facts

- About 40 percent of CO_2 emissions in the United States result from electricity production.
- About 20 percent of CO_2 emitted into the atmosphere comes from the gasoline burned in motor vehicle engines.

Save Electricity

lectricity is generated from both nonrenewable and renewable sources. However, most of the electricity used by the world is produced by burning coal in thermal power plants. Thus, to prevent the harmful emissions of GHGs, we need to save electricity.

Save for the Present

At present, the global demand of electricity exceeds its supply by a great margin. In fact, more than 1.3 billion people in the world still do not have access to electricity. Moreover, they have to deal with an increasing number of power cuts due to less supply. It is therefore important that we stop taking electricity for granted, and start saving it as much as we can to equalize its demand and supply.

Why Save Electricity?

The electricity generated by burning fossil fuels is the cheapest and the most reliable source as compared to that generated from other sources. Saving electricity will not only reduce electrical pollution but also bring down electricity bills.

Save for the Future

By wasting electricity, we are wasting **precious** fossil fuels, which will **ultimately** be exhausted if we continue to use them at the present rate. Due to overuse, future generations will have to completely depend on renewable sources for electricity generation. Thus, we must use electricity wisely and find **efficient** alternative methods of electricity generation for the future.

Saving electricity

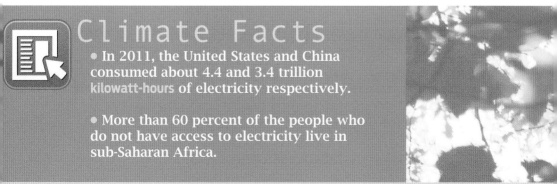

Climate Facts

- In 2011, the United States and China consumed about 4.4 and 3.4 trillion kilowatt-hours of electricity respectively.

- More than 60 percent of the people who do not have access to electricity live in sub-Saharan Africa.

Save Fuel

Every day we use fuels to run vehicles and motors, and to cook food. Fuels are derived from crude oil—a nonrenewable resource. Once used, it cannot be regenerated in a short period. Thus, it is important to use oil judiciously and look for alternative options that would be more **sustainable**.

Reduces Oil-dependence Costs

More than half of the world's oil reserves are located in the Middle East. Therefore, they have the power to dictate oil policies. The other countries have to pay the price decided by the Middle Eastern countries for each barrel of oil. Thus by saving fuel, the other countries can save a lot of money.

Controls Climate Change

When fuel is burned in vehicles, harmful greenhouse gases are emitted, which intensify global warming. If less fuel were used, there would be fewer emissions, which would, in the long way, help to control climate change caused by global warming.

Helps Animals

The pollution caused by the harmful emissions of vehicles affects the health of humans and animals. Whereas humans protect themselves from this pollution by seeking shelter in their homes, small animals are forced to bear the dire effects of pollution. Saving fuel is important so that animals can breathe freely and live a long life.

Climate Facts

- From 2014 to 2018, world oil demand rose from 94.2 million to nearly 100 million barrels per day.

- In the United States, gasoline and diesel together make up about 84 percent of all of the energy used for transportation.

A Looming Oil Crisis

More than 87 percent of the world's energy is generated from fossil fuels. Out of this, about 40 percent is derived from oil alone. Such heavy dependence on oil to meet energy needs and its unchecked use indicates that an oil crisis is looming over us.

Effects of Oil Shortage

Oil and natural gas are used to produce **fertilizers** and **pesticides**. Without oil, their production would suffer, which would ultimately lead to a decline in food grain production. Even the prices of other manufactured goods would increase **steeply** as their transportation would suffer due to oil scarcity. Technology-intensive institutions such as health care will also have to bear the brunt since tons of medicines and plastic disposables are made using petroleum. Oil shortage is also leading to growing concerns about "energy safety" in countries that import most of their oil. The most oil-rich region in the world is the Middle East—a region that has become unstable due to foreign intrusion, weapons' deals and political manipulation by countries that are not as oil-rich.

Predictable Future

Countries such as Saudi Arabia, Canada, Iraq, Iran, Kuwait, the United Arab Emirates, Russia, Venezuela, Mexico, the United States, and a few others have the world's oil reserves. A growing number of these nations are reaching their oil-producing capacity. In the near future, oil production will decline while the demand will continue to increase. Then the oil-producing countries will sell oil to the other countries on their own terms, while the oil-importing countries will have to compete with each other to get oil.

70% of oil demand grow from petrochemic

The future of oil

Climate Facts

- The United States consumes 20 percent of the world's oil. As of 2018, only about 11 percent of that was imported, the lowest total since 1957.

- The Middle East has enough oil to last 88 years at the present production rates.

Energy and Recycling

There is a very close relationship between energy and the goods we use in our everyday lives. Goods such as electronics, batteries, toys, bottles and many household goods such as carpets and curtains are produced, processed, and transported using energy. To save energy, we must recycle such goods.

Recycle

When we recycle any item, we keep it from turning into waste and going into **landfills**, where waste is burned and harmful gases are released yet again. Thus, by recycling goods, we save the energy that was used to manufacture them as well as prevent more harmful emissions. The products that are made of recycled goods use 30 percent less energy in their production.

How recycling saves energy

Three Rs

- **Reduce:** Reduce the usage of energy by switching off appliances when not in use and by using energy-efficient products only.
- **Reuse:** By reusing products, we save all the energy that has been used to manufacture them. It is better to reuse a glass than to throw it away since it would take about one million years for that glass to break down and **decompose** in a landfill.
- **Recycle:** By recycling products, new items can be made from the old ones using less energy as compared to the energy used in making a new product. Copper wiring, newspapers, aluminum cans, and glass containers are some popular recycled items.

Climate Facts

- The energy saved in recycling a single aluminum can could power a television for three hours.

- The recycling process of plastic uses only a tenth of the energy required to make new plastic from raw materials.

Paper Pollution

The production, manufacturing, and transportation of paper require a huge amount of energy, which creates paper pollution. Paper is so widely used that recycling it is a must to control paper pollution. Paper recycling will also cut down on the overuse of wood pulp from trees.

Paper Production

Almost 17 watt-hours of energy (Wh) are used to produce a sheet of paper. In comparison, recycled paper uses less energy (around 12 Wh) and almost half the water normally needed to manufacture one sheet from fresh wood pulp. Recycling a ton of paper can save up to seventeen trees. At the same time, during the production of paper, waste products such as dimethyl sulfide, the highly toxic total reduced sulfur compounds (TRS), and volatile organic compounds (VOCs), such as methanol gas, are released and endanger the environment. American scientists have invented a technology that recycles the methanol wastes and converts them into methyl formate—a blowing agent and solvent that is environment-friendly.

Use Both Sides

A normal, medium-sized **copier** copies about fifty pages per minute and uses about one thousand watts of energy. This is equal to the energy used in the production of one sheet of paper. Obviously, the production cost of a single sheet is much more than required in copying or printing. Thus, we must copy or print on both sides of the paper to save energy. This would also result in less paper pollution.

Reduce Paper Consumption

Buy notebooks or diaries made of recycled paper only. Prefer buying **unbleached** and uncolored paper. Buy paper in bulk as it reduces the packaging, which again uses energy in its production. Print only if it is very important. Stop using paper cups and use your own glass.

Climate Facts

- Paper accounts for more than half of the total municipal solid waste.

- One ton of recycled paper saves 3,700 pounds (1,678 kg) of lumber and 24,000 gallons (90,950 l) of water.

Trees Save Energy

Forests cover about 30 percent of the land surface. Trees are an essential part of the biosphere. They provide oxygen for living organisms to breathe. A big, leafy tree can provide a day's oxygen for about four people. Trees also reduce soil erosion and help us in various other ways. Therefore, we need to protect them.

Reduce Air Pollution

CO_2 emitted by factories, automobiles, and the burning of fossil fuels is one of the main causes of air pollution. Trees absorb CO_2 for preparing their food with the help of photosynthesis, thus reducing the content of this potent GHG. They also clean air by absorbing other air pollutants such as sulfur oxides, nitrogen oxides, etc. This is how they help in decreasing air pollution and global warming.

Impact of trees on conserving energy

Trees Save Energy

Trees keep the surroundings cool through the process of evapotranspiration. They absorb water through their roots and evaporate it through the pores of their leaves. Pavements made of asphalt absorb more light energy and heat the air above them. On the other hand, light-colored pavements reflect light energy toward the buildings around them. Therefore, planting more trees in residential areas would help reduce heat and reflection. Trees also provide shade that reduces solar radiation and helps houses and buildings stay cool on hot days. This cuts down the need for electricity to power air conditioners. In the winter, trees prevent the extremely cold winter winds from entering houses. This saves the energy required by room heaters to warm houses.

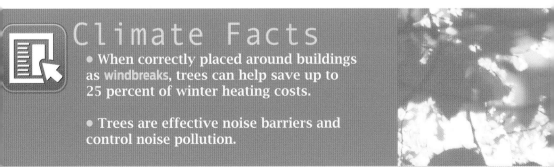

Climate Facts

- When correctly placed around buildings as windbreaks, trees can help save up to 25 percent of winter heating costs.

- Trees are effective noise barriers and control noise pollution.

Save Water, Save Energy

Thermal power plants make use of water to generate electricity. On the other hand, energy is required to pump, treat, and transport water all over the world. In both processes, harmful gases that cause global warming are released into the atmosphere. Thus, we must save water and in turn save energy.

Spend Less

When we conserve water, we automatically reduce the consumption of energy that goes into processing and transporting it. Moreover, by using water-efficient appliances that require less water, we cut down our water bills as well. Hence, saving water not only saves energy but money too.

Water Labeling Systems

Many countries such as Australia, Singapore, the United States, and the United Kingdom have developed water-efficient labeling systems for the plumbing fixtures with the help of the International Association of Plumbing and Mechanical Officials (IAPMO). Water efficiency in plumbing can be practiced by managing the output of water in different plumbing fixtures. Water-efficient labeling in developing countries such as India is still in the evolutionary stages. The IAPMO along with the Indian Plumbing Association (IPA) has developed a water rating proposal known as Water Efficient Products–India (WEP-I) to rate Indian plumbing fixtures, including faucets, dish washers, and clothes washers.

asy Ways to Save Water

- For shaving, use a mug rather than running water.
- Close faucets while soaping and rinsing clothes.
- Upgrade older toilets with water-efficient models.
- Operate automatic washing machines and dishwashers only when they are fully loaded.
- Water your garden during early morning or late evening, to reduce evaporation.

Climate Facts

- Almost 60 percent of a household's water footprint can be used for lawn and garden maintenance.
- The power plants in the United States use 136 billion gallons (514 billion l) of water each day.

Threat to Wildlife

Global warming is changing the breeding and reproduction patterns of almost all wildlife species. To avoid extinction, living organisms are trying to adapt to the changing environment. Various energy-related projects such as the construction of hydroelectric dams, wind turbines and mining projects disrupt wildlife and damage their ecosystems.

Dams and Power Plants

The construction and operation of hydroelectric dams around the world have **endangered** many marine organisms, especially fish. Dams obstruct the path of many ocean-going species such as salmon when they go to spawn in the rivers where the babies are born. It also poses a problem for baby fish, which seek a way back to ocean and seas. Water usage in nuclear and fossil power plants also hurts marine animals. Many power plants discharge untreated, heated water from their once-through cooling (OTC) systems into rivers and coastal water bodies.

Wind Farms: Loss of Habitat

A large number of birds and bats are injured or even die by colliding with the blades of wind turbines. The construction of large wind farms spreading over several acres of land causes loss of habitat. It can also cause many birds to change their foraging grounds and migration routes. Birds and bats also have to use extra energy to fly across huge wind farms. By slowing down the blades of wind turbines, when wind speeds are lowest at night, a large number of bats and birds can be saved.

Mining Threat

Mining has disturbed the nesting sites, foraging grounds, as well as the distribution of wildlife. Surface mining releases acid-forming materials, which threaten reptiles, burrowing animals, small mammals, and others. Indian tigers are in danger due to excessive coal mining. A large number of coal mines and coal-run power plants have come up in India in the past five years. This has affected the tiger population in many areas such as Chandrapur, Maharashtra.

Climate Facts

- Around 1,706 tigers live in India, which is more than half of the world's tiger population.

- Every year, as many as four hundred forty thousand birds die accidentally by coming into contact with wind turbines in the United States.

Energy Efficiency

nergy efficiency is achieved by using technology that utilizes less energy to perform the same function. Many countries have developed energy efficiency programs that rate different appliances by giving them energy stars according to their energy efficiency. The higher the number of energy stars, the greater the appliance's energy efficiency.

Energy Efficient Products

- **Fluorescent bulbs:** Compact fluorescent light bulbs use only one-third of the energy used by a standard incandescent bulb to produce the same amount of light. They last ten times longer and generate 70 percent less heat.
- **Refrigerators:** Energy star refrigerators consume 75 percent less energy than those manufactured in the 1980s.
- **Clothes washers:** Energy star washing machines use 50 percent less energy than the other standard models. These machines use only 18-25 gallons (68-95 l) of water for a full-sized load, compared to the 40 gallons (151 l) used by standard washers.
- **Room air conditioners:** An energy star air conditioner reduces energy consumption by 20-50 percent and cuts down energy bills by a high percentage.
- **Home electronics:** Energy stars on home appliances indicate that they use less energy. Use ink-jet printers, as they are more energy efficient than laser printers. Also, LCD televisions and monitors use less power than CRT or plasma screens.

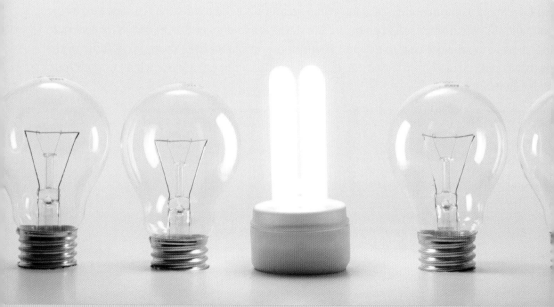

Energy Labels

Most countries use two types of energy labels: comparative and endorsement. Comparative labels are designed to allow the consumer to determine the energy efficiency as well as compare the rankings of all products that carry a label. Comparative rankings are voluntary in some countries. Common comparison labels use a scale with neatly defined efficiency categories.

Endorsement labels are generally used for the most energy efficient class of products, or for those that meet a fixed eligibility criterion. Such products generally carry a mark or logo, which shows that the required standards are met. They may carry little or no comparative information at all.

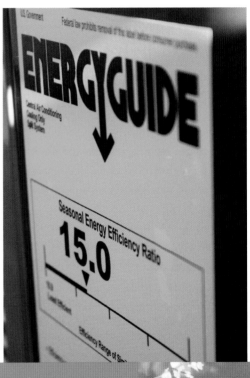

Climate Facts

● Only about 10 percent of the energy used by a bulb creates light; the remaining 90 percent creates heat.

● Refrigerators with freezers on top use 10–15 percent less energy than a side-by-side model of the same size.

Smart Meter

A smart meter is an electric meter that measures the amount of electricity used and indicates the time of the day when it is used. These meters are being used in many countries like Italy, Canada, Japan, the United Kingdom and others. Their popularity is growing worldwide.

Time-of-Use Pricing

Electricity prices change over the course of the day, depending on the demand and the supply of power.

- **Off-peak** is the time when the demand is low and the less expensive sources of electricity are used. Off-peak time is usually from 7:00 p.m. to 7:00 a.m. in both summer and winter.
- **Mid-peak** is the time when the demand as well as the cost is moderate. It is usually from 5:00 p.m. to 7:00 p.m. and 7:00 a.m. to 11:00 a.m. in summer and from 11:00 a.m. to 5:00 p.m. in winter.
- **On-peak** is the time when the demand is the highest and more expensive forms of electricity production are used. It is usually from 11:00 a.m. to 5:00 p.m. in summer and from 7:00 a.m. to 11:00 a.m. and 5:00 p.m. to 7:00 p.m. in winter.

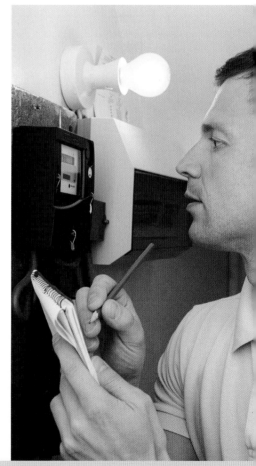

Benefits

During peak hours, when demand is high, electricity is derived from nonrenewable energy resources. These resources cause pollution during electricity generation. To reduce pollution, users need to time their electricity use to mid-peak and off-peak hours when it is less expensive. By reducing electricity consumption during peak hours, electricity bills can be brought down.

30 Million Smart Meters in the U.S.*

How do smart meters work?

Climate Facts

- In Italy, more than thirty million consumers use smart meters.

- In December 2009, the United Kingdom's Department of Energy declared that it would install smart meters in all homes by 2020.

Saving Energy at School

Young students can also join the fight against global warming. Saving energy in schools is beneficial for all of us. Schools can safeguard our future by educating students about the need and benefits of saving energy since they would follow the same measures at their homes and elsewhere.

Energy Consumption

On average, about 55 percent of the energy in schools is used for heating and cooling the school building. About 20 percent is used for lighting, 15 percent for catering, and the remaining for computing and other purposes.

Energy Team

Energy can be saved by keeping a check on the unnecessary wastage of energy. Teachers could organize an energy team of students who would monitor the use of lights and electrical equipment in classrooms. They should report to the teacher if there is any wastage of electricity.

Energy-saving Measures

- Turn lights off when the classroom is empty.
- Use natural lighting whenever possible.
- Install "Occupancy Sensors." They will automatically turn off the lights when no one is in the room.
- Switch off appliances such as the classroom computer and printer when not in use.
- Put up awareness posters and reminder stickers next to switches in the classroom.
- Ensure all windows are closed while the heating or cooling is on.
- Use an adjustable **thermostat** and turn it down and up according to the need.

Climate Facts

- Lighting costs could be reduced by up to 15 percent by turning off lights when leaving a room.
- By implementing energy-saving measures, schools can easily cut down about 20 percent of their energy costs.

Ways to Save Energy

t is up to everyone to do what they can to save and preserve energy. The process has to start small, with every household and family, and expand into every block, town, city, and state. Here are some ways that you and your family can try to preserve energy today.

1. Install a programmable thermostat to adjust temperature according to need.
2. Reduce heating in unused rooms in the house—close doors and heat registers, too.
3. Remove any obstructions and clean heating registers regularly.
4. Replace furnace filters, once a month, during the heating season.
5. Seal doors and windows with caulk and plastic film.
6. Replace single-pane windows with energy-efficient double-pane windows mounted in nonconducting window frames.
7. Turn off the lights when not in use.
8. During sunny winter days, close curtains and shades at night, and keep them open during daytime.
9. Improve the insulation of your home.
10. Dust lighting fixtures to maintain illumination.
11. Use fluorescent bulbs.
12. Control outdoor lights with sensor timers so they stay off during the day.
13. Replace a gas-cooking appliance with an automatic electric ignition system.
14. Use microwave ovens since they consume 50 percent less energy than conventional gas stoves.
15. Turn off electric stoves several minutes before the specified cooking time.
16. Use flat-bottomed pans that make full contact with the cooking coil.
17. When cooking on a gas burner, use moderate flame settings to conserve LPG.
18. Use pressure cookers as much as possible.
19. Use lids to cover the pans while cooking.
20. Minimize the use of kitchen, bath, and other ventilating fans, or install a timer to switch them on.
21. Always purchase energy star models of electrical equipment. They are energy efficient.
22. Turn off your home office equipment when not in use.
23. Turn off the monitor of your computer during your breaks from work.

24. Unplug battery chargers after use; they continue to draw power if they are plugged in.
25. Maintain the refrigerator at 35–40°F (1.6-4.4°C) and the freezer section at 0–5°F (-17 to -15°C).
26. Choose a refrigerator/freezer with automatic moisture control.
27. Regularly clean and dust out the coils behind or under your refrigerator with a tapered appliance brush.
28. Make sure your refrigerator door seals are airtight.
29. Do not open the doors of the refrigerators frequently.
30. Allow hot food to cool before placing it in the refrigerator.
31. Thaw frozen foods in the refrigerator.
32. Always wash clothes in the washing machine only with full loads.
33. Always use cold water in the rinse cycle.
34. Choose natural drying over electric dryers.
35. During the summers, open windows at night to bring in cool night air; close them during the day.
36. Prefer air conditioners having automatic temperature cut-off.
37. Cook in a microwave. It creates less heat and humidity in homes.
38. Clean your air conditioning unit's condenser of dirt and debris.
39. Seal the doors and windows properly when the air conditioner is switched on.
40. Install solar reflective film on windows.
41. Run the dishwasher only with a full load of dishes.
42. Air dry dishes in a dishwasher.
43. Use a manual lawn mower.
44. Use energy-efficient appliances.
45. Repair leaky faucets.
46. Reduce the temperature setting of your water heater to warm.
47. Install low-flow showerheads.
48. Use a single high-watt bulb instead of a number of low-wattage bulbs.

1. What does the text say is the most widely used form of energy?

2. Name three types of renewable energy.

3. Where does the text say is home to a quarter of the Earth's undiscovered oil?

4. Name two of the nations that text says are major oil producers.

5. What are two ways to cut down paper use, according to the text?

6. How are wind farms harmful to some wildlife?

7. Name one of the possible energy-efficient products people can add to their homes.

8. What is a smart meter?

1. Find out what your household's monthly electricity bill is. Then examine the list on the previous page and other tips from the text. Put as many of them as you can into practice. After a month, see how your electricity bill is affected. Did it go down? If so, why do you think it did?

2. Electric or gas-powered car? Research the pros and cons of both and prepare a chart that compares them. What are the advantages of electric cars? What are the disadvantages? Which type of car would you choose?

3. Help spread the word! Research the facts about energy conservation and make a poster that encourages and instructs people how they can help . . . and how they can do more! Use colorful graphics and attention-grabbing stats to make your case.

FIND OUT MORE

Books

Johansen, Bruce. *Examining Energy and the Environment Around the World.* Goleta, CA: ABC-CLIO, 2019.

Reddy, B. Sudhakara, and Gaudenz B. Assenza, Dora Assenza, and Franziska Hassemann. *Energy Efficiency and Climate Change: Conserving Power for a Sustainable Future.* Thousand Oaks, CA: Sage Publishing, 2018.

Washburne, Sophie. *Alternative Energy Sources: The End of Fossil Fuels.* New York: Lucent Books, 2018.

On the Internet

Energy Facts and Stats (U.S. agency site)
www.eia.gov/energyexplained/index.php?page=about_energy_efficiency

Sciencing: Tips on Conserving Energy
sciencing.com/conserve-energy-daily-life-2327.html

More Tips!
www.homeselfe.com/100-ways-to-save-energy/

bioaccumulation the process of the buildup of toxic chemical substances in the body

biodiversity the diversity of plant and animal life in a habitat (or in the world as a whole)

ecosystem refers to a community of organisms, their interaction with each other, and their physical environment

famine a severe shortage of food (as through crop failure), resulting in hunger, starvation, and death

hydrophobic tending to repel, and not absorb water or become wet by water

irrigation the method of providing water to agricultural fields

La Niña periodic, significant cooling of the surface waters of the equatorial Pacific Ocean, which causes abnormal weather patterns

migration the movement of persons or animals from one country or locality to another

pollutants the foreign materials which are harmful to the environment

precipitation the falling to earth of any form of water (rain, snow, hail, sleet, or mist)

stressors processes or events that cause stress

susceptible yielding readily to or capable of

symbiotic the interaction between organisms (especially of different species) that live together and happen to benefit from each other

vulnerable someone or something that can be easily harmed or attacked

INDEX

Photo Credits